UNRULY BLOOD

Olivia Douglass is a British-Nigerian writer, poet and artist. A Barbican Young Poets Alumni, they self-published the pamphlet *Slow Tongue* in 2018. Olivia was shortlisted for the Rebecca Swift Foundation Women Poets' Prize 2020, and was the winner of the Guardian and 4th Estate 4thWrite Prize 2022 with their short story *Ink*. Olivia has an MSt in Creative Writing from the University of Oxford, and writes across multiple genres and forms.

First published in 2024 by Little Betty, an imprint of Bad Betty Press
Cobden Place, Cobden Chambers, Nottingham NG1 2ED

badbettypress.com

Copyright © Olivia Douglass 2024

Olivia Douglass has asserted their right to be identified as the author of this work in accordance with Section 77 of the Copyright, Designs and Patents Act of 1988.

PB ISBN: 978-1-913268-68-8
EPUB ISBN: 978-1-913268-69-5

A CIP record of this book is available from the British Library.

Book design by Amy Acre
Images by Olivia Douglass

Unruly Blood

OLIVIA DOUGLASS

LITTLE BETTY

CONTENTS

Efe is my other name / fathers call / other life / my free body	9
playground	12
him	13
maternal	14
swell	15
we nearly made it out alive	17
us that hide from touch	18
pronoun	20
love interludes	21
ripe	24
can I we really be all this !!!!	27
Notes	34
Acknowledgements	35

I measured time differently,
with all my body.

Annie Ernaux

what was
done has
been is
still
doing

in us
I we

never undone

echoing

Efe is my other name / fathers call / other life / my free body

Efe Efe Efe my fathers tongue handed a na( )me I have never claimed
I am born be( )longing in the weight of flesh

Efe in a place (   ) I am

efE Efe efE Efe
rolling song swaying something un(   )catched

(*Efe*   ) has come again
heard my blood trying to turn to water
sighs at such desires   knows the taste of them

he calls   *Efe oh oh Efe ohh oohhh*
in his mouth I am kept
from ( ) wandering

he sings *Efe Efe oohh Efe*

me ungrown
collapse onto carpet
after dancing in circles to his ( ) naming
little chest not yet heavy pulsing in prayer

Efe come

carry me ( )　　　　there
again　　　　　　　　　　before they come
　　　with moulding hands

take me
away
　　　　　where you (　be)

　　gently and true

E feeee E feee E ffff eeeeee

then
a tickle in my ear stroke of wet　almost breath
small hairs stand still　craning

Efe has come again

playground

white kids plunge their hands through my hair
        I slip out   across the   hopscotch

one with blue eyes yellow curls   wants me to chase her
                                                                           so I do

behind the big gate I give her my small tongue she takes
my mouth
    I want this   to never name itself   or be caught

bells ring   our mums talking of tea   play

saturday we make a den   & I wriggle all over her
in pyjamas
        I feel   everywhere   inside me   become

by monday lunch owen is her new boyfriend
                                          & the whole class knows

he is really good at football   she tells people   they will
get married when they are older

                I can run fast too   I can kick hard

him

out the door as if never coming back
& this time   never comes back
that first night without
instinct still pulls four plates for food

no no

how do girls like me grow
if not in his image
voice unbreaking   new chest groans heavy each day
walk into a lean like he does

after your being gone
what did I have to make of myself
but a gentle   yearning thing
both daughter & sun

maternal

what is in her
is in me
I want ~~rid~~
I want

swell

true. I am filling with past.
each night the moon calls for her water
& so it comes. I too rush up the staircase
pull the door &
break into no light.

tell us
how to empty a flooded body or
bring bodies back from liquid graves.
erode me   soften me steady.
what is lost in the waves
cleanses now.

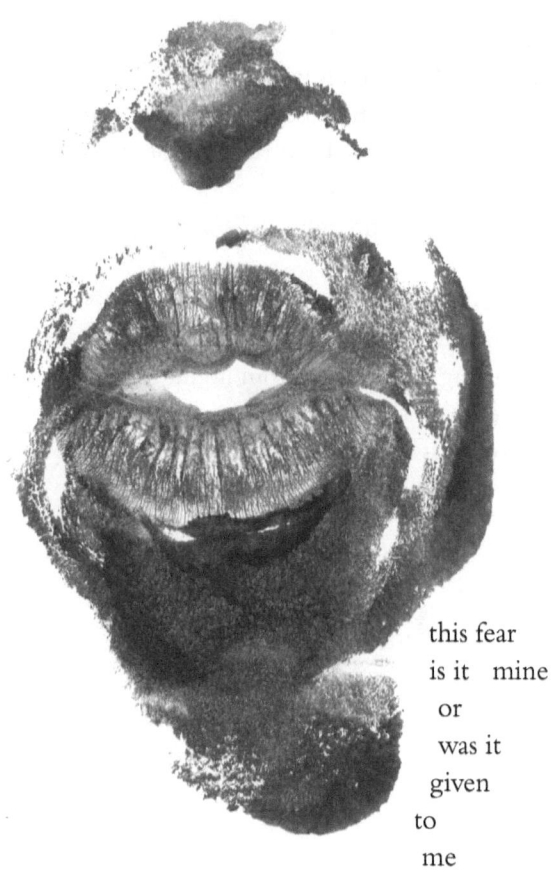

this fear
is it   mine
or
was it
given
to
me

we nearly made it out alive

look! outside the sun flashes green.
old tears come like birth waters. wet the ground.
then from the carpet. shoots of pink grass.
you were born with hair everywhere   reaching
over your forehead   even connected to your eyebrows

wet faced   lighter now
no more nights spent embryonic. coiled underneath
the kitchen table the bed the sky.
wanting nothing to touch us.
you would scream endlessly   I could not put you down
for a second   you have always been stubborn

first the house wobbled like a tooth.
now the walls crash
down. naked   lay waiting in the new garden for a future
as long as light to spill into us.
something in you so alarmed   to be alive

& even still a whisper untangles itself
I feel therefore I can be free
thereforethereforhere
an otherwise life
& in it joy is breaking everywhere

look!

us that hide from touch

home as dark space
bed sheets skin which binds breath to us

curled inside
you unfold me   pull out from behind my ear

I submit under the weight of fingertips
the air is black blue   bending

where?

me learning to undress myself   me
whose veins carry the blood of prey

in darkness   I am not found   nor my palms
that float to shadows   plant themselves there

air black   blue   womb dark
reminds me to be in it in it in it   grow myself again

here?

this unlit   this mess of us
this reaching rib   a sprouting stem

call me something to be safe in
& come to always

you strum my chest gentle
whirl around the room crawl back

like this?

I pull panting parts close
whisper into them   passing secrets

through wet   open   hand moving inside
I am summoning a new name for myself

pronoun

I won t answer for this assigned language
. No.

when you say I just get confused, it's not grammatically
correct
& grammatically correct makes our air thick

I think
.yes &
that too   could be

beautiful
that you might call me in multitudes
that I might come in my thousands   &

what punctuation. would you put, ?here
here.   where a chest protrudes   into a life sentence,

love interludes

23:48 Paris

>we waited long for daylight to go
>   to become gone   here
>if we can call the black water
>of my back stretched out   a place
>holding your image wavering
>like the reflection of a moon

>I swear nobody on land has been
>this delicate
>where your hand is pressing
>   mylovemylovemylove
>a yolk is forming   andand
>you sink in me   I run with you

15:12 Camden

>kiss skips
>down my back   guessing
>where your mouth
>might land   lose count
>of the next the next &
>
>next one

06:02 Athens

        so
        daylight has come
        to wrap me around you

        makes a morning of us
        dream clings like dew

        bodies flowering
        into singing colour

02:53 Peckham

        swaying in any which way
        eyes might catch me
        yes   this young   & brazen
        yes   me
        just another fruit getting ripe
        under the sun of somebody   &
        though I could twist towards
        endless arms let the pulp swell give
        it to anyone
        I won't

00:00

       my ear at the pulse
       spinning out from your chest
       like a left record
       play me only this

beat
 after
      beat

   after

beat

ripe

there I was all up in it ripening years twisted
into oiled locs all loving each living inch all
over kissed over fire I gave thanks for these
loyal bones green fingers the rolling night all
wine all wonder mirror caught my body twirling
out of sage smoke I was all ready kneading
the song soil sweat of it knowing nothing of a
binary bondage a bountiful mess of myself
everything under the sun is changing all the
time all my skin soft lovers flocking to the
river all the water leads to my centre filling
slowly with true there I was all set in my
ways all blooming

When, at once, pale-skinned and rushing in,
they came. All mouth and muttering. Spouting
something about lifting me up, out, elsewhere.
Talking about my voice space and their voice
space, how they are learning it all from books I'm
in. Thick white smoke and promise lies. Of course,
they came with coins too, all shiny, well kept, ready
to be thrown. Came talking about something,
looking for what

I sat holding all my things stared stared stared
did not lift a finger

still each day is new light to be born into
      again   again   & again

can I we really be all this !!!!

I know   I am a language!
       or at least   a
green patch   on which foreign   becomes found

the   words here at this page   are   of course
 the most docile   ones that   hung low   & let ink take them
easy   unlike   other

unruly truths   which set   ablaze   in me
a black smoke   straying from
the faltering   flames of   tongue

              I don't need
to be articulated!   I just want   to lick
the head of my oblivion   until no new born   wounds grow

★

*

    I keep a picture of myself under the bed. I am a child, around three years old, & it is christmas time. Stood alone at the centre of the room, in front of the tree & television. Wrapping both small hands around a gold bauble, which I hold to my belly. I have my mum's attempt at bantu knots fixed together by multicoloured ties, that look as if grown from the lights & tinsel behind. Two tiny hoops hang from each ear, gifts from *granny in Africa*. My face is round & open in the way that a field is open. In one look, my lips are about to curve into beaming smile, in another they are pouting. I am staring directly into the lens as if through the lens & back of the camera through the palm of whoever is taking the photo through their chest to the back wall of the room through that to the fuchsia in the garden   & through each twig   each part of air   each blue of sky   through the thin wet skin   of the world   to some strange otherwhere a kind of look that holds its knowing palm up to the glass.

*

★

if asking
you got me?

I am echoing back
of course   my baby   over   & over   again

★

★

      I can sometimes   trace my lineage

              of sounds
birth waters fall   choir of playgrounds

                  uhhh
    ksskis   kisskisskiss

      air cry   wave break

   salt   bug sing   *came this country*
         when I was your age

r&b spinning   itch of eczema skin

   road hummmm   bd   aaa
          domino yawning
              new page stroke   suck teeth

  when I grow, I want to be   ee

                  spitting stew
                  keys clicking like rain

soft thud in flesh   kisskskisiss   yells swelling under
              floorboard
uuhh   sssh
  secrets rustling in ears   soggy mud hop
      4 3 2 1 ready or not

  bed bumping   through the black

★

*

Looking right at us, face as stunned as a bullseye. To hold this photograph is to hold you. Is to remember that you are always a reason. & how should I explain this here where I   we are found? Is it enough to say safe or known? Instead, if it is possible that in one look you are standing alone, then it is possible that in another we both appear in the picture. I come out from behind the tree & curl over you, a bow. My chin rests on your head, we stare directly into the lens. I cover your eyes with my palms with the lightness of two leaves floating on water. We walk drifting past the camera & whoever is taking the photo & out through the garden towards gaping blue strange new   air   stirring wonder &   soon my hands   open

*

!!!!

★

I am   a   party!
   dizzying the night
with   surprise

my ballooned   heart strung   spinning
 scatters the light   on memory   so it
  becomes   dancefloor

& now   in every   movement
life is   coming!
 sure as   blood

★

NOTES

The prints in this book are created by Olivia Douglass, and are impressions of the writer's body using acrylic and ink.

In 'swell' the line 'bring bodies back from liquid graves' echoes M. NourbeSe Philip's 'What is the word for bringing bodies back from water? From a 'Liquid Grave'?' in 'Notanda', from *Zong!*.

'we nearly made it out alive' directly borrows language from Audre Lorde, 'The white fathers told us: I think, therefore I am. The Black mother within each of us – the poet – whispers in our dreams: I feel, therefore I can be free', from *Sister Outsider: Essays and Speeches*.

The line '& in it joy is breaking everywhere' is a nod to Gboyega Odubanjo's poem titled 'There Is Joy Breaking Here'.

ACKNOWLEDGEMENTS

Thank you Gboyega Odubanjo. Deeply loved, forever with us.

Huge appreciation for the Bad Betty team for bringing this book into being. Many thanks to the editors & staff of the publications in which early versions of these poems have appeared: *bath magg*, *Nothing Personal*, *Montez Press*, *National Poetry Library*, *FEMZINE*.

With endless gratutide for my family, friends and teachers.

www.ingramcontent.com/pod-product-compliance
Lightning Source LLC
Chambersburg PA
CBHW030312100526
44590CB00012B/613